STARK LIBRARY   JUL   2021

# KEVIN HART

# KEVIN HART

CARLA MOONEY

Rosen YA
New York

Published in 2020 by The Rosen Publishing Group, Inc.
29 East 21st Street, New York, NY 10010

Copyright © 2020 by The Rosen Publishing Group, Inc.

First Edition

All rights reserved. No part of this book may be reproduced in any form without permission in writing from the publisher, except by a reviewer.

### Library of Congress Cataloging-in-Publication Data

Names: Mooney, Carla, 1970– author.
Title: Kevin Hart / Carla Mooney. Description: First edition. | New York : Rosen Publishing, 2020. | Series: The giants of comedy | Audience: Grades 7–12. | Includes bibliographical references and index.
Identifiers: LCCN 2018054371| ISBN 9781508188735 (library bound) | ISBN 9781508188728 (paperback)
Subjects: LCSH: Hart, Kevin, 1979-—Juvenile literature. | African American comedians—Biography—Juvenile literature.
Classification: LCC PN2287.H26 M66 2020 | DDC 792.7/6028092 [B]—dc23
LC record available at https://lccn.loc.gov/2018054371

*Manufactured in China*

**On the cover**: Kevin Hart has curated an entertainment empire, with himself as the centerpiece; he is shown here at a movie premiere in 2016.

# CONTENTS

6    Introduction

10    **CHAPTER ONE**    Cracking Jokes to Cope

22    **CHAPTER TWO**    Lil' Kev

34    **CHAPTER THREE**    Breaking into the Business

44    **CHAPTER FOUR**    I'm a Grown Little Man

54    **CHAPTER FIVE**    Breakout Success

66    **CHAPTER SIX**    Hollywood Superstar

77    **CHAPTER SEVEN**    I Can't Make This Up

88    Fact Sheet on Kevin Hart
89    Fact Sheet on Kevin Hart's Work
93    Critical Reviews
95    Timeline
97    Glossary
99    For More Information
102    For Further Reading
104    Bibliography
108    Index

# Introduction

In October 2016, comedian Kevin Hart got emotional as he was honored with a star on the Hollywood Walk of Fame. "I don't get here without you and without your support. I am a representation of what you have made me. I love you all. Thank you so much. Today is an honor," Hart said at the Walk of Fame ceremony according to ABC7.com. The star was given in the category of live performance, and recognized Hart's incredible talent and career as a comedian, actor, author, and businessman. Hart attended the ceremony with his blended family, including his wife, Eniko Parrish, ex-wife Torrei Hart, daughter Heaven Hart, and son Hendrix Hart. Many friends—including his *Ride Along* costar Ice Cube and manager Dave Becky—were also present at the ceremony.

Hart's star on Hollywood Boulevard is next to a DSW Shoes store, which is fitting, because the comedian began his comedy career while he was working as a shoe salesman in his hometown of Philadelphia, Pennsylvania. Since his days selling sneakers, Hart has gone on to become one of

Hollywood's biggest talents. Mike Berkowitz, comedy department head at APA Agency, has been Hart's touring agent since 2008. He told *Variety*'s

Kevin Hart is shown here posing for pictures as he is honored with a star on the Hollywood Walk of Fame in 2016 in Hollywood, California.

Iain Blair that he knew Hart was a special talent from the moment they met. Berkowitz said:

> I was always a fan of his TV and film work and back then he was better known for that than his standup, which was just beginning to sell. We met through a mutual friend, and I fell in love with Kevin the moment we sat down, and knew it'd be a great partnership. Not only is he extremely talented, but he's shockingly motivated and as determined as any artist I've ever met, and he's also not afraid to think outside the box and put himself out there.

On stage, Hart is loud and rambunctious. His comedy is often physical: he prowls and paces across the stage, plays with the microphones, and uses theatrics to entertain his audience. He can be loud and change his voice in a split second, going from a high-pitched whine to a low growl at the drop of a hat. Yet perhaps the thing that makes Hart so popular is his ability to relate to his audience. He talks about his childhood, failed relationships, and parenting struggles in ways that everyone can understand. Through his stories, Hart's fans see that the comedian is a regular person—just like them. Hart told Emily Zemler of *Esquire:*

# Introduction

Your fan base can only grow if there's a strong sense of authenticity to go behind it. I have that. I'm not fake or phony. This isn't a façade. What you see is what you get. The personality of Kevin Hart is the same personality that you think it is from what you've seen on TV, in stand-up, in interviews. I don't change.

From his humble beginnings in Philadelphia, Kevin Hart has become one of the funniest—and most successful—men on the planet. From starring in blockbuster movies to headlining sold-out stadium shows, Hart has accomplished much in his career, and he has no plans of stopping any time soon.

# CHAPTER ONE

# Cracking Jokes to Cope

On July 6, 1979, Kevin Darnell Hart was born in the City of Brotherly Love—Philadelphia. He was the second son born to Nancy Hart and Henry Witherspoon. During Kevin's childhood, his father struggled with drug addiction and drifted in and out of jail. This left his mother, Nancy, to raise Kevin and his brother, Robert Kenneth Hart, primarily on her own. Hart's experiences during these formative years helped to mold him into the man and comedian that he is today.

## A Strong Role Model

As the primary provider for her sons, Nancy Hart worked as a computer analyst for the University of Pennsylvania. Money was tight, and the little family lived in a tiny, one-bedroom apartment

# Cracking Jokes to Cope

The downtown skyline of Philadelphia, Pennsylvania, was a familiar sight for Hart as he spent much of his childhood in the city.

in North Philadelphia, one of the city's toughest neighborhoods. Their apartment was so small that Kevin and his brother slept in a bunk bed in the hallway. Although they did not have much, Nancy did her best to make it a home for her boys.

Nancy always pushed her sons to work hard. She told them to set goals for themselves and then go about achieving them. She followed her own example perfectly: during Hart's childhood, she constantly pursued education to make a better life for her sons. "She was forever in school," Hart told *Variety*'s Brett Lang. "She was always trying to get a new level within her education—a new master's or a new degree. She was constantly pushing to be the best version of herself." Nancy's hard work did not go unnoticed by her son. Today, Hart credits his mother for developing his terrific work ethic and diligent attitude.

## A Troubled Father

When Hart was a child, his father struggled with drug addiction, using heroin and cocaine. Witherspoon also spent a lot of time in jail for various offenses. His drug use and unreliability—such as the time he dropped a young Kevin off at the wrong school—forced Nancy to limit the time Witherspoon spent with her sons.

While Hart's father was missing for much of Hart's childhood, his brother, Robert, who is eight years older, often stepped in as a father figure for his younger brother. "My dad was crazy," Robert told *Rolling Stone*'s Jonah Weiner. "Kevin was too young to know that the [stuff] was as dysfunctional as it was." However, there were many times that Robert could not shield Kevin from their father's problems. Once, Kevin and his brother were walking with their dad when a group of young men attacked Witherspoon. As the boys stood shocked, the men began to beat up their father. Between punches, Witherspoon calmly told the boys to go home and wait for him. About an hour later, Witherspoon strolled home covered in blood to greet his terrified sons. He did not mention the fight and simply asked if they wanted something to eat. Another time, his father showed up at Kevin's school spelling bee high on drugs and rooted for his son like he was at a raucous sporting event. When Hart was about twelve years old, Witherspoon pointed to a young man Kevin did not know and told him it was his brother, Omar. At first, Hart did not understand what his father meant; he eventually realized that his father had children with another woman, one of whom was Omar.

Watching his father screw up time after time left a lasting impression on Hart. Witherspoon became a role model of sorts for Hart—a role model of what not to do. Hart told Brett Lang from *Variety*:

> He didn't escape any of it—jail, drugs, addictions, ruining your family to a point where

my mom didn't want me and my brother to be around him. Seeing the stuff firsthand. Seeing the reality behind drugs and addiction, and what it can really do to a person, that's why I don't do drugs. I learned what I shouldn't be doing from what my dad did.

Later in life, Hart was able to reconnect with his father. Still, he never forgot his father's behavior during his childhood. His experiences would eventually become part of the material he used on

## FORGING A NEW RELATIONSHIP

Today, Hart and his father have reconciled and formed a new relationship. After years of struggling with substance abuse problems, Witherspoon is sober and Hart has often said that he has forgiven him and holds no hard feelings about the past. Hart believes that it is important for his children to have

Cracking Jokes to Cope

After a difficult childhood, Hart and his father have formed a healthy relationship as adults. Shown here from left to right are Robert Hart, Halle Berry, Henry Witherspoon, and Kevin Hart.

a relationship with their grandfather, partially to make up for his own lack of relationship with the man. Witherspoon makes an effort to talk to Hart's children regularly. He sends them messages and video chats with them, making sure that he is present in their lives in a way that he was not able to be for his own son.

stage, and some of his most beloved bits are tales about his father's wild actions.

## Class Clown

Growing up, Hart learned to rely on his sense of humor to cope with his family life and classmates. At school, Hart became the class clown, which made him popular with his peers and kept him from being picked on because of his short stature. From a young age, he understood that he needed to accept himself—being angry about not being taller would not prevent him from being bullied. Instead, as he wrote in his memoir *I Can't Make This Up: Life Lessons*, "You can be the funny guy and accept your size. An added incentive for choosing the latter is that it's hard for someone to punch you while they're laughing. I chose to be the funny guy." Comedy also became his shield to keep him out of trouble in his tough neighborhood. "Nobody wants to fight the funny guy. Nobody wants to mess with the funny guy. Everybody wants to be around the funny guy. And that's what I was," he told Tracy Smith from CBS News.

At school, Hart was an average student at best. He preferred cracking jokes and playing basketball to studying. His mother also signed him up for the school's swim team to keep him busy and out of trouble. During his senior year of high school, Hart

**Cracking Jokes to Cope**

Standing next to Shaquille O'Neal at the Beverly Hilton Hotel in 2013, it is easy to see Hart's trademark small stature.

received a minor award at the swim team banquet and stepped up to give a speech. For the next fifteen minutes, he told self-deprecating jokes and had the whole room laughing. "I didn't know I was doing stand-up, but in retrospect, it was my first comedy set. … I was the star of the banquet," Hart wrote in his memoir. Afterward, people came up to Hart and his mom and congratulated him. His mother begrudgingly admitted that Hart's speech was good. Yet at the time, Hart did not realize that

## ROLE MODEL: EDDIE MURPHY

One of Kevin Hart's early role models in comedy was the legendary comedian Eddie Murphy. When he was a child, Hart remembers one day when his mother was out and his cousins were visiting. He could hear them laughing hysterically as they watched a video. Hart peeked around the corner and saw a man dressed in vibrantly red leather: It was Eddie Murphy performing in *Eddie Murphy: Delirious*. Hart's cousins could not contain their laughter. Hart had never seen a movie where just one person spoke, alone on stage. This was one of his first impressions of a stand-up comedian's art.

After starting his comedy in the 1970s, Murphy broke into the mainstream when he joined the

**Cracking Jokes to Cope**

One of Hart's role models in comedy, Eddie Murphy is shown here performing a stand-up show at the Comic Strip in New York City in 1984.

*(continued on the next page)*

# KEVIN HART

*(continued from the previous page)*

comedy television show *Saturday Night Live* (*SNL*) in 1980. He was known for both his original characters and his impersonations of other entertainment stars, including James Brown and Stevie Wonder. He has also starred in several hit films, including *48 Hours* (his first), *The Nutty Professor*, and *Dr. Dolittle*.

Murphy's stand-up comedy was known for being full of profanity and including sketches and impersonations of a wide range of people. In 1984, his second stand-up comedy album, *Eddie Murphy: Comedian*, won a Grammy for Best Comedy Album. In 2016, Murphy was presented with the Hollywood Career Achievement Award at the 2016 Hollywood Film Awards.

his talent for making people laugh could turn into a career.

## Hart's College Experiment

In 1997, Kevin graduated from George Washington High School. His mother insisted that he continue his education. With her help, he registered at the Community College of Philadelphia for summer classes. He planned to get his grades up at this school before transferring to a larger college to play basketball.

At the community college, Hart tried out for the basketball team. Even though he was small, he was confident about his playing ability. To his surprise, however, he did not make the team. At the collegiate level, his short stature was simply too difficult an obstacle to overcome.

Meanwhile, his college classes were not going well either. He felt like school just was not for him. So without telling his mother, Hart began applying for jobs at local retail stores. He landed a job as a shoe salesman at a City Sports store in Philadelphia. The manager handed Hart a pamphlet and told him to memorize it. He needed to know everything about the store's sneakers because the customers expected expert service. The job would end up changing Hart's life.

A few days after he was hired at City Sports, Hart broke the news to his mother that he was dropping out of community college. She warned him that he could not just hang around doing nothing. He reassured her that he needed some time to figure out what he wanted to do with his life—and in the meantime, he would work. Reluctantly, Nancy Hart agreed.

# CHAPTER TWO

# Lil' Kev

Within a few weeks of working at City Sports, Hart was charming customers and making sales. Hooked after receiving his first sales commission check, Hart asked for longer shifts at the store. After a visit from a Nike sales representative, Hart announced to his mother that he had finally figured out his life plan—to work for Nike. He put all his energy into work, often taking triple shifts and working holidays and birthdays. He became known in the store as the guy with all the energy.

Soon, customers stopped by the shoe department just to see Hart. He had a way of making people feel better if they were having a bad day. Before long, Hart's hard work paid off: he was promoted to floor general and given a raise.

At City Sports, Hart entertained his coworkers with his humor, often pretending to be different characters when selling shoes to customers.

One day, a coworker suggested that he think about doing comedy as a second job. She told Hart about a comedy club called the Laff House near the store where people got on stage and told jokes. Hart agreed to try it. When the other store employees found out that Hart was going to try stand-up comedy, they told him he would be fantastic. Their confidence in him helped motivate him to follow through on the idea.

## Taking the Stage on Amateur Night

Hart called the Laff House and asked if they had any openings for new comedians. The woman who answered told him about the club's amateur night held every Thursday—anyone could perform, they just had to sign up.

As Hart prepared for his first amateur night, a friend asked him what stage name he was going to use. The friend explained that most comedians used a stage name, from Cedric the Entertainer to Sinbad. Hart decided to go with Lil' Kev. Over the next few days, Hart tested jokes on customers and coworkers. He practiced day and night, often turning anything from his day into a joke. He filled his pockets with paper scraps on which he had written joke ideas. When he ran into a friend, he would pull out one of the scraps and try out the joke on him or her.

# KEVIN HART

An amateur comedian is shown here telling jokes and practicing his stand-up routine in front of an audience at an open mic night. Hart got his start in comedy the same way.

When the day of the show arrived, Hart was nervous. He had not been on stage since the swim team banquet in high school. He worried that everyone would just stare at him in silence. When his name was called, Hart ran onto the stage and launched into his overenthusiastic act. He was so nervous that he flew though his five-minute routine in only three minutes and had to add a few extra jokes at the end. Although the performance was not perfect, the audience laughed. The feeling of being on stage hooked Hart immediately. In only five minutes, he had fallen in love with stand-up comedy.

The week after his first performance, Hart returned to the Laff House for another set. This time, though, he was more familiar with the club and how amateur night worked. Because he was more comfortable, his routine went even better. At the end of the evening, the manager announced that the club was changing the amateur night format. It would now be a competition judged by the audience, and the winner would take home a $75 prize.

The next week, Hart performed in the club's amateur competition. Even though it was only his third performance, Hart beat out all the other competitors. The win fueled his drive to be the best stand-up comedian he could—his hobby was turning into his passion. During the week, he would work on new jokes to use at the next competition. After his third win, Hart began taking comedy more seriously. He stopped working triple shifts at City Sports and used the extra time to go to the club and watch professional comics. He noticed that their performances were more than just jokes—they also presented a crafted appearance on stage.

## Taking a Chance on Comedy

With some local success under his belt, Hart realized that he wanted to pursue stand-up comedy full-time as a career. He quit his job at City Sports. Breaking the news to his mother was difficult, but she agreed and promised to support him for a year while he tried to make it in the industry. If he could not, then she wanted him to go back to school. His mother gave him a check for his next month's rent. She also handed him a Bible and instructed him to read it.

Now able to fully devote himself to comedy, Hart traveled around the Philadelphia area, performing in different venues and gaining experience on stage. Whenever he was not on stage, Hart worked on his Lil' Kev persona. He wanted to create the most fun, high-energy five-minute performance he could. People began to notice the new kid, and many thought he had potential. After a few weeks, the Laff House manager gave him a five-minute guest spot on a weekend show—a much higher-profile performance than he was used to.

Unfortunately, though, Hart's work was not bringing in a lot of money. That left Hart struggling to make ends meet. His mother had promised to help with rent, but he was a month behind. When he asked her about the rent, she asked if he had read his Bible yet. When he was two months late on rent, the landlord put an eviction notice on Hart's apartment door. Again he asked his mother about the rent. She asked if he had read his Bible. He had not. Frustrated, Hart went home and opened the Bible for the first time since his mother had given it to him. Inside, he found rent checks for the entire year. He called his mother and apologized.

# ANECDOTAL AND OTHER TYPES OF COMEDY

Hart's style of comedy frequently uses anecdotes to make the audience laugh. An anecdote is a narration of a humorous and interesting event—in other words, a story. When used for comedy, the anecdote is generally personal, which can be either true or partially exaggerated. Anecdotal comedy is a very popular type of comedy. Other comedians who are known for this style of comedy include Louis C. K., Dave Chappelle, Bernie Mac, Jim Gaffigan, and Chris Rock.

*(continued on the next page)*

*(continued from the previous page)*

Comedian Jim Gaffigan is shown here performing on stage at the Hilton New York in 2018. Gaffigan is known for his anecdotal comedy.

Though Hart and other prominent comedians use anecdotes to make audiences roar with laughter, there are dozens of other kinds of comedy as well. Jerry Seinfeld made a name for himself through observational comedy, while Tig Notaro has had success with her deadpan delivery and Demetri Martin delivers classic jokes, with a set-up and a punch line.

## Gigs Around Town

For the next year, Hart performed gigs all around town, in clubs, restaurants, bowling alleys, and community centers. When *Def Comedy Jam* hosted a competition at the Laff House, Hart signed up. *Def Comedy Jam* was an HBO television series produced by Russell Simmons, an entrepreneur and record producer. The show had launched the careers of several prominent black comics. Excited for the opportunity, countless comics from Philadelphia signed up for the competition. Hart won the event and landed an opening slot on the *Def Comedy Jam* tour when it later came through Philadelphia.

Suddenly, Hart was not the new guy any more. Comedians who had never talked to him congratulated him, and Hart was booking every show he could to get more stage time to prepare for the *Def Comedy Jam* show.

A few weeks before the *Def Jam* show, Hart stopped by the Laff House to see a local comedian named Keith Robinson perform. Robinson was an experienced and respected stand-up comic and actor. He agreed to give Hart a guest spot, opening for his show that night. Hart went on stage, and every joke he delivered was a hit, keeping the audience laughing.

KEVIN HART

Comedian Keith Robinson, one of Hart's early mentors, performs a stand-up routine at the Stress Factory Comedy Club in New Brunswick, New Jersey.

After the night's performance, Hart asked Robinson what he thought of his show. Robinson told him it was awful. Robinson explained that Hart's show was just a replay of old, corny jokes that had been done before. Hart was not letting the audience see who he really was; nothing in the set was personal. Robinson advised him to stop doing what he thought the audience wanted and to work on being his own comedian. He also told Hart to drop the "Lil' Kev" stage name.

Stung by the criticism, Hart stayed to watch Robinson's performance. He noticed that the entire routine was about Robinson's life, his family, and his point of view. Robinson told real, detailed jokes about his mother and brother. The entire time, he appeared relaxed on stage. Rather than playing a character, Robinson was simply sharing his own funny personality with the audience. While watching him, Hart realized that Robinson was right—he was trying too hard.

## Trips to New York City

Robinson took Hart under his wing and invited him on a trip to New York City, the comedy capital of the world. In New York, Hart watched Robinson perform show after show at different clubs. Hart returned with Robinson numerous times. Each time, he watched Robinson's performances in several venues. During one of the trips home, Robinson talked to Hart about his material. Robinson told Hart that he needed to find something from the heart—something that mattered. He told Hart to look at how influential comedian Richard Pryor was able to find the funny in his everyday life and turn it into a routine that people loved.

A neon sign glows near the Stand Up NY Comedy Club in New York City. In his early career, Hart studied comedians as they performed in New York clubs.

Hart took Robinson's advice and began performing as Kevin Hart. Because he was so used to being the Lil' Kev clownish character on stage, he struggled being himself at first. Sometimes, he was booed off the stage. While he was perfecting this new, authentic act, Hart continued to travel with Robinson to New York several times a week to watch and learn from his performances and those of other comedians. Each time, Robinson pointed out how the comics on stage constantly refined their sets with every performance. Hart realized that Robinson was right, and he had a lot of work to do to get to that level. He needed to think about rewriting and reshaping every phrase in his act and concentrate on every nuance in his performance. As he worked to sharpen his act in his Philadelphia shows, Hart tried to concentrate on what was naturally funny about himself.

Robinson was relentless in his feedback, and Hart listened to him. He started taping his shows in Philadelphia and reviewing each performance. He also began using some of his own real life experiences as the basis for his jokes. The whole time, he was beginning to find his niche.

# CHAPTER THREE

# Breaking into the Business

Once Hart changed his style on stage, Robinson thought he was ready to take the next step in his career. Robinson began introducing him to New York City comedy club owners to prepare him for auditions. The first audition Hart landed was at the Boston Comedy Club. He was already familiar with the venue because he had been to it dozens of times with Robinson to watch other comics. He passed the audition and earned a five-minute spot on Sunday nights. Hart soon passed auditions at several other clubs, including Stand Up NY and Gotham Comedy Club. Before long, Hart was performing regularly in New York, sometimes as many as five shows a night. He constantly hustled to get spots and book performances wherever he could. All of that hard work was starting to get him noticed by people in the industry.

## Getting Personal

As Hart's career started to take off, Robinson continued to urge him to get more personal with his material. He pointed out that Hart was still making up jokes and instead of sharing his own real experiences. Robinson advised Hart to talk about stuff people could relate to, including his very real troubles with his girlfriend Torrei.

At first, Hart was hesitant to share these details of his life in public. After giving it some thought, he decided to push himself. The next time he went on stage, Hart told a roomful of strangers about a recent fight he had with Torrei. The audience laughed through the entire story, and Hart finally understood what Robinson had meant about letting the audience get to know him. Instead of just trying to crack made-up jokes, Hart could use the painful parts of his life and transform them into stories that could touch—and possibly help—others. He realized that the audience was not laughing at the jokes; instead, they were laughing at his reactions and his delivery.

After that revelation, Hart began looking at his life and what was happening around him in a new light.

## FIRST MARRIAGE

While at Community College of Philadelphia, Hart began dating a young woman named Torrei. As he pursued his dream of stand-up comedy, Torrei moved with him to Los Angeles, California. Their relationship was often tumultuous, with the couple frequently getting into loud, explosive fights. In 2003, however, Hart and Torrei married and would eventually have two children: Heaven Leigh and Hendrix Kevin. As Hart traveled to pursue his career, Torrei built a home for the family. However, the constant fighting and separation took a toll on the marriage. The couple split in 2010 and were divorced in 2011. Despite their romantic relationship breaking down, Hart and Torrei still try to maintain a healthy parenting relationship. Both are highly invested in making a great life for their children, and they work together to make sure they can provide that.

Kevin Hart met his first wife, Torrei Hart, in Philadelphia in the early days of his career. They had two children together before eventually divorcing in 2011.

Breaking into the Business

His performances began to include more material about situations that he actually experienced and his reactions to them. Incorporating more personal stories paid off, and he began to book consistent headlining gigs in New York.

## Just for Laughs and More

In 2000, scouts for the Just for Laughs Festival in Montreal, Canada, saw Hart perform in New York and offered him a spot on their New Faces showcases. Just for Laughs was one of the biggest comedy festivals in the world, and everyone important in the comedy industry would be in attendance—including club promoters, television executives, and film casting agents. Doing well at the festival could launch any comedian's career, even potentially landing him or her a part in a television

Howie Mandel performs at the Just for Laughs Comedy Festival, one of the biggest events in the comedy industry.

show or movie. Despite this enormous opportunity, Hart's manager at the time advised him to hold off and work another year on his material. He took that advice.

A year later, in 2001, Hart was invited again to perform in the New Faces showcase. This time, he was ready. He did very well in his two performances, and the festival's bookers added Hart to every event where they had extra space. When Hart returned from Montreal, his manager used his success to set up meetings with directors, casting agents, production companies, and television networks.

In 2001, Hart was invited to audition for *Saturday Night Live*, the weekly television show that had launched the careers of countless comedians, including Eddie Murphy and Chris Rock. Though he performed well at the audition, he was passed over for another comedian named Dean Edwards. "We were sure he was gonna get it, but ... the other guy got it. The first thing Kevin did was to call him and say congratulations. He's had ups and downs, but he's never complained—he's just kept working," said his manager, Dave Becky, to *Rolling Stone*'s Jonah Weiner.

As Hart was making more of a name for himself in stand-up circles, he caught the attention of Damon Dash, the cofounder of Roc-A-Fella Records with Jay Z. Dash noticed Hart at one of his shows

**Breaking into the Business**

Damon Dash, cofounder of Roc-A-Fella Records, recognized Hart's comedic talent and encouraged him to expand his career into film.

in 2002 and later offered him a role in an upcoming indie movie. Dash also wanted Hart to work with a few other comedians to write the movie script for the film, which would be an urban crime comedy. After two months, the script for *Paper Soldiers* was finished and Hart started filming with the rest of the cast. While filming, Dash encouraged Hart to improvise during many of his scenes. Just a few weeks later, the filming was done, and Hart returned to the New York comedy circuit. Although the film was not a financial success, it opened doors for Hart as an actor.

When a young director named Judd Apatow told Damon Dash that he was looking for a young black comedian for a new television pilot, Dash told him about Hart. Hart flew to Los Angeles, California, to meet with Apatow. Hart nailed the audition and landed a part in a show, titled *North Hollywood*, about three struggling roommates living paycheck to paycheck in California. The cast included Judge Reinhold and two other young, little known comics: Amy Poehler and Jason Segel. They shot the pilot in seven days and Hart returned to New York. Although ABC did not pick up the pilot, another break was right around the corner for the burgeoning Hart.

Apatow—who is now known for his many off-the-wall mainstream comedy films—went right back to directing and creating television shows after the failed *North Hollywood* pilot. One of his early successes was a show on Fox titled *Undeclared*, which was centered on college students. He offered Hart a small role across three episodes in 2002—and Hart accepted. Though this show fizzled out after a single season, it gained a reputation among loyal viewers.

## Writing His Own Material

After his first appearances on screen were funny but unsuccessful, Hart's luck changed. He landed a few small roles in different movies, including *Scary Movie 3* (2003) and *Along Came Polly* (2004), starring Ben Stiller and Jennifer Aniston. In the horror movie parody *Scary Movie 3*, Hart landed the part of CJ. At first, the role was small, but the director expanded the role for Hart and asked him to write some of his scenes into the script. While filming the movie in Vancouver, Hart had a revelation. He realized that his television appearances had not been successful because it was not his material. If he wanted the next venture to succeed, he needed to write it himself.

When he returned home, Hart began to develop a television series loosely based on his family. *The Big House* featured Hart as a wealthy, spoiled young man who is forced to go live with distant family in a poor Philadelphia neighborhood after his mother passes away and his father goes to prison. ABC liked the idea and gave Hart the green light to tape a pilot episode. After watching the pilot, ABC ordered twelve episodes of the sitcom in 2004. Despite early positive signs, the show's storyline never took off with audiences, and ABC cancelled it after only six episodes.

KEVIN HART

> Though *Soul Plane* had a star-studded cast, including hip-hop legend Snoop Dogg (*left*), the movie was considered a commercial failure.

After *The Big House* disappointment, Hart turned his attention to another project. He had landed the lead role of Nashawn Wade in the movie *Soul Plane* (2004). The cast included Tom Arnold, Snoop Dogg, and Method Man. Though there was a lot of hype and anticipation for the film, *Soul Plane* was a box office flop, earning only $13.9 million in the United States.

## On the Road

Tired of waiting for network executives and casting agents to call in Los Angeles, Hart decided to start touring again and performing his stand-up routine. He traveled around the country, performing in small clubs and on college campuses. "I've been to some of the damnedest places for comedy," Hart told *Rolling Stone*'s Joshua Weiner. "I performed in a place in Atlantic City called Sweet Cheeks … I performed at family dinners, family functions … You name it: All shots to my pride have been taken." By performing live stand-up, even at less-than-desirable venues, Hart got back to his roots and worked on his craft.

These experiences helped Hart when he was asked to perform in a *Comedy Central Presents* stand-up special in 2004. The half-hour episode was a small preview of the self-deprecating comedy that Hart would later become known for, making jokes about his height and family that fans loved.

# CHAPTER FOUR

# I'm a Grown Little Man

Whenever he was in Los Angeles between stand-up tour dates, Hart continued to audition for small parts in movies and television. He landed several small roles in films, including *The 40-Year-Old Virgin* (2005), *Fools Gold* (2008), and *Meet Dave* (2008). Meanwhile, the work Hart put into his stand-up was paying off. His manager, Dave Becky, believed that he was ready to do an hour-long television special. Hart called Eddie Murphy, who he had met on the set of *Meet Dave*, for advice. Murphy had starred in the first comedy special Hart had seen as a child. Now, Murphy told Hart to trust himself and his own way of doing things and forget about advice from others. With these words of wisdom, Hart felt ready to do the show.

*I'm a Grown Little Man*

In 2009, Hart released his first stand-up special, *I'm a Grown Little Man*. In this one-hour Comedy Central set, Hart was a ball of energy, constantly pacing across the stage. Throughout the show, Hart poked fun at himself, touching on topics from his short stature to his drama-filled relationships. He used a variety of voices to mimic ordinary people in everyday situations. *I'm a Grown Little Man* became one of Comedy Central's highest-rated specials and solidified Hart as a serious stand-up talent.

Hart poses with comedian Eddie Murphy, one of his comedic idols, at an event in West Hollywood, California, in 2011.

## Life Changes Provide New Material

For his stand-up sets, Hart continued to draw from his personal life for inspiration. Some big changes in his life provided new material—most notably, the birth of his two children. In 2005, Hart's wife, Torrei, gave birth to their first child, Heaven Leigh

# KEVIN HART

Hart. Their son, Hendrix Kevin Hart, was born two years later in 2007. On stage, Kevin joked about having two kids. Some of his most popular bits included him complaining about all the difficulties associated with fatherhood. Though there are definitely challenges to being a parent, Hart played up how much it annoyed him for the crowd. Offstage, Hart has admitted that he sees himself as a fun dad—at least most of the time.

Hart's children with his first wife—Hendrix and Heaven—give him great comedic material on a daily basis.

"I'm a fun dad until you don't do what you're supposed to," Hart explained in a *People* magazine interview. "But even the tough dad is still fun because I can't not laugh at myself for trying to be tough!"

Around the same time, Hart's relationship with Torrei worsened. The couple constantly fought, particularly over the time Hart spent away from home. He felt trapped in an unhappy marriage with an angry wife. He also struggled to pay the

# COMEDY CENTRAL

In 1989, the media company Time Warner launched The Comedy Channel. It was the first cable channel focused exclusively on providing comedy-based programming. Soon after, MTV launched its own comedy channel, Ha!, which featured sitcoms and short comedy skits. After two years, the two channels merged to become Comedy Central. Today, Comedy Central broadcasts original, licensed, and syndicated series, stand-up comedy specials, and feature films geared toward a mature audience. Comedy Central plays in nearly ninety-two million households across the United States.

bills, despite becoming a bigger and bigger star. Many people in his audiences shared these real-life problems, which made them compelling material for his show. Though he felt trapped in his relationship with Torrei, he was free when he was telling stories for the crowd. Each set he performed was a little bit therapeutic. When talking about the problems in his marriage, Hart was careful not to humiliate Torrei. Instead, he made himself—his actions and his reactions—the butt of his jokes. Being so relatable made Hart's comedy better, and he landed more gigs because of it. However, this turned into a vicious cycle. The more bookings he got, the worse things got with Torrei, which made his comedy better, and the cycle repeated.

## Making Marketing Work

As he traveled the country doing show after show, Hart also worked hard to connect with fans. After each show, he asked fans for their email addresses. He gave each a flyer with his picture, a tagline from the show, and information about him. By doing this, he hoped the people would remember when he came back. He also directed fans to Myspace—the hot social media site at the time—which allowed him to target and send messages to audiences by geographic region and let fans know about shows coming to their area.

Hart's efforts to market himself and his shows paid off. He started getting larger crowds in cities where he had performed before and made a marketing push. Fans came back for a second show because they liked him so much. People told him that they loved his material. Even more importantly, fans started buying tickets in advance for his shows—this increased the clubs' revenues and allowed Hart to demand more money when he came back. After all, the quicker a comic can sell tickets, the faster the owners of a comedy club can make money.

Today, Hart uses social media to pull in fans and promote his tours. He has more than thirty million followers on Twitter and more than sixty million followers on Instagram. He has become a marketing machine, using social media to tweet and post about his movies, shows, and tours.

## A Significant Loss

While Hart's career was taking off in the mid-2000s, he suffered a significant loss in his personal life. In 2007, he flew to Australia to film a big-budget action movie, *Fools Gold*, starring Matthew McConaughey and Kate Hudson. Before Hart left for Australia, Hart's mother was diagnosed with ovarian cancer. Although she had never attended one of his stand-up shows, Nancy was a fierce supporter of her son. She kept her cancer diagnosis a secret from Hart as long as possible because she wanted him to focus on his career. However, Nancy's health continued to deteriorate, and his brother called Kevin in Australia to break the bad news. As soon as Hart found out, he booked the next plane to Philadelphia to visit his mother.

Over the next few weeks, Kevin traveled back and forth between Australia and Philadelphia, trying to balance work and spending time with his mother. As the cancer progressed, Nancy insisted that she wanted to stop chemotherapy treatment and go home. She passed away in 2007 while Hart was on set in Australia. With permission from the film's producers,

Hart returned home to make arrangements for her funeral. He knew that his mom had wanted her suffering to end, and he realized that being hurt or angry about her death would not change anything. He still thinks about his mother a lot, and her advice and support keep him motivated every day.

After his mother's funeral, Hart and his brother cleaned out her belongings. They discovered a box of memorabilia that she had saved from both of their careers. For Hart, his mother had saved videotapes of *The Big House*, newspaper clippings from his performance at Just for Laughs, and advertisements for his performances at the Laff House. In fact, she had saved almost every ad and article about Hart. She had never mentioned her collection to Hart, and he was surprised and touched at how closely she had been following his career. It gave him the confidence to keep working hard and achieve success in show business.

## Seriously Funny

As Hart's stand-up career continued to climb, his club dates sold out regularly. He began to perform two shows a night in many cities. Promoters noticed the number of tickets he was selling and offers for comedy tours rolled in. Hart turned them all down. Instead, he booked the Allen Theatre in Cleveland, Ohio, to tape his second stand-up special, *Seriously*

## I'm a Grown Little Man

*Funny*. In 2010, the stand-up special debuted as Comedy Central's highest rated special of the year. *Seriously Funny* was also released as an album and DVD on Comedy Central Records in 2010. The album went quadruple platinum, meaning it sold more than four million copies.

In the meantime, Hart also continued to appear on screen. He landed roles in big-name movies, including *Little Fockers* (2010) with Robert DeNiro and *Death at a Funeral* (2010) with stars Chris

In 2010, Hart starred with actors Danny Glover, Martin Lawrence, and Tracy Morgan (*left to right*) in the film *Death at a Funeral*.

Rock, Tracy Morgan, and Martin Lawrence. He also hosted Black Entertainment Television's (BET) classic stand-up comedy series *Comic View: One Mic Stand*.

In recognition of his rising popularity on stage and screen, Hart was asked to host the 2011 BET Awards show. The Black Entertainment Television network established the BET Awards to recognize African Americans and other minorities in acting, music, sports, and other entertainment fields. "When we asked folks who should host this year's BET Awards online, in the streets, among other celebs and throughout social media, one name came back to us loud and clear: Kevin Hart," said Stephen Hill—BET's president of music programming and specials—according to an article by Ahmaad Crump of WZAKCleveland.com. "He is blue flame right now, and we are looking forward to working with him on the show. His energy, wit and the always-fantastic performances will make for yet another must-see event."

## The End of a Marriage

While pursuing his career ambitions, Hart's relationship with his wife, Torrei, continued to suffer. Though they had often butted heads and fought in the past, Kevin's long hours on the road made arguments a constant occurrence when he came back home. Eventually, in 2010, the couple reached a breaking point; they separated in that year, and officially divorced in 2011. Hart filed for and received joint custody of their children. In a 2016 interview with talk show host Chelsea Handler, Hart admitted that he carries some of the blame for his failed marriage. Hart told Handler:

> I was young on my first marriage, Chelsea. I'm not ashamed to say it, guys. I got married at the age of 22. I was still all over the place. I didn't really understand the definition of marriage. I wasn't ready for it, so I take responsibility. I can say I messed my first marriage up. I'm man enough to say that.

Still, Hart has maintained a strong relationship with his ex-wife since the divorce and the pair work together to coparent their children. Though their split was caused by serious and continual disagreements, their postmarriage life has been—if not positive—at least respectful. Both Torrei and Kevin are committed to being present, active parents for their two children. Hart, especially, is motivated to be a good father because his father was not there for him.

## CHAPTER FIVE

# Breakout Success

All the turmoil in Hart's personal life—though challenging—became a treasure trove of new material for his shows. For the first time, he was willing to dig deeper into his life and share some of the more personal moments about his family and his father's struggles with addiction. For a comedian who was becoming known for not being afraid to bare his soul, Hart knew that he needed to share the parts of his life that he had kept hidden in the past. He knew the stories were funnier than anything he could have made up himself—and if he did it right, when he left the stage, people would understand who he was.

### Opening Up Onstage

To test his new material, Hart performed in unscheduled spots in New York clubs.

Sometimes, there were only a few people in the audience. At each venue, he tried different stories and approaches. Sometimes, he would be on stage for long stretches without a laugh. Other times, he noticed people in the audience checking their phones. Though some people might be disheartened by these failures, Hart knew that he needed to bomb before he could succeed. If he could find a way to win over audiences in a tough room, then he would have no problem in a venue packed with people who actually wanted to see him.

Hart found that as he opened up and talked about the difficult parts of his life, the immediate response of audience laughter told him that they related to his experiences. Even further, delivering jokes and stories about his personal trauma was beneficial to his mental state. Though audiences do not talk back to the performer at stand-up shows, Hart was—in some ways—going through a public therapy session by airing out his grievances and mistakes in front of a live crowd. As many other comedians have found, this is very helpful. The more he shared about his personal life, the more Hart began to heal.

The material he developed from these deeply personal subjects became Hart's Laugh at My Pain tour. In 2011, Hart took off on a ninety-city tour that made him a household name. The comedy tour earned more than $15 million in ticket sales, making it one of the most successful comedy tours in history. On the Laugh at My Pain tour, Hart also broke Eddie Murphy's long-standing record for the first black comedian to gross more than $1.1 million in ticket sales for a two-day live comedy show. In an interview with the *Columbus Dispatch*, Hart talked about the tour:

> It's called "Laugh at My Pain." I talk about my trials and tribulations in my everyday life. The purpose is to put out the pains that hurt me, now that I'm in a place where I talk about it … My fans relate to it, I think, because they feel they know me … Comedy gives some healing when you relate to real life, marriage, kids, turmoil … Laughter heals all wounds.

On stage, Hart engaged his audience and won them over with his direct honesty. The show also launched one of Hart's best-known lines, "All right, all right, all right," which he repeated frequently throughout the show to hilarious effect.

## Taking a Risk

Instead of recording one of his shows and selling it to Comedy Central—as he had done in the past—Hart wanted to do something new with this

Breakout Success

## PLASTIC CUP BOYZ

The Plastic Cup Boyz are a trio of comedians—Will "Spank" Horton, Na'im Lynn, and Joey Wells—who frequently open for Hart on his comedy tours. Hart met each of the Boyz early in his career. In his memoir, Hart describes them as his "fellow road warriors." Together, they played at bars, clubs, and other venues, and bonded over their experiences while touring nonstop. For many shows, Wells hosted, Spank opened, Na'im featured, and Hart closed. They toured as an entire ensemble. It worked well for the clubs because they could book entertainment to fill and entire night in one shot. For audiences, the group put on a consistent show night after night, and many of the gags and bits followed a similar theme.

tour. He decided to release his recorded show as a stand-up theatrical film. Comedy greats, including Eddie Murphy and Richard Pryor, had made similar comedy films, and Hart wanted to follow in their footsteps. He filmed two live shows at the Nokia Theater in Los Angeles, so that he would have a backup of every joke.

In 2009, Hart formed a production company: HartBeat Productions. He rented office space in

Ventura, California, and invested the money he was making on tour into producing his comedy special. It cost him quite a bit of money, but it was worth it: he owned everything fully outright and retained all the rights for distribution. He took a risk by putting in the money upfront—but if the film succeeded, he would also be able to reap all the rewards for himself.

Hart and his producing partner for the special, Jeff Clanagan, tried selling the film to studios in Hollywood. At first, everyone passed on it. In response, the pair decided to distribute it themselves. They took it to AMC Theaters and it was picked up immediately. HartBeat Productions self-distributed *Laugh at My Pain* exclusively in AMC theaters. They created prints, shipped them to the theaters, made posters, and took care of all the marketing themselves.

When all was said and done, Hart and HartBeat were out a lot of money. If the movie tanked, it could be the end of a budding comedy career. However, the risk paid off. In its opening weekend in 2011, *Laugh at My Pain* grossed nearly $2 million at the box office. It was the tenth-biggest film that weekend—a rare feat for a stand-up comedy film with a limited release. AMC added more screens the following weekend, anticipating even greater success. *Laugh at My Pain* went on to gross nearly $8 million at the box office. According to

Box Office Mojo, it was the ninth-highest-grossing stand-up comedy film of all time. "I think it was a pivotal moment in comedy," Clanagan said to Kris Frieswick of *Entrepreneur* magazine. For Hart, he was no longer just a star, but he had also become a successful businessperson. "If Kevin wants to do something, he's not afraid to invest in himself, because he understands what his brand is. You couldn't go to 90 percent of the people in Hollywood and ask them to invest in their own movie," Clanagan explained.

When *Laugh at My Pain* was released as a DVD in 2012, it sold very well. Overall, *Laugh at My Pain* confirmed Hart's talent as a comedian and cemented him as one of the industry's best upcoming performers. Not only was he becoming a household name for his comedy, he was also demonstrating his considerable talents in the business world.

## Hollywood Comes Calling Again

Meanwhile, Hart was offered a leading role in an upcoming romantic comedy movie, *Think Like a Man*, based on comedian Steve Harvey's book of the same name. The ensemble cast also featured Michael Ealy, Jerry Ferrara, Meagan Good, Regina Hall, Terrence J., Taraji P. Henson, Romany Malco, and Gabrielle Union. When filming, the director encouraged Hart to follow his instincts and improvise his own humor into his scenes. Many of those improvised lines and jokes made the movie's final cut. When filming wrapped, Hart was optimistic. After many box office flops, he thought this film had a good chance to succeed. When *Think Like a Man* hit theaters in April 2012, it soared to number one at the box office on opening weekend with $33.6 million in ticket sales. Overall, the movie was an incredible success and grossed $96 million worldwide.

With Hart riding the wave of success on both stage and screen, Hollywood came knocking at his door. Producers wanted to meet with Hart to discuss about new projects and ideas. Journalists wanted to interview the rising star. He even landed a recurring role on the hit sitcom *Modern Family*.

In recognition of his popularity, MTV invited Hart to host the 2012 MTV Video Music Awards. While Hart's BET Awards show appearance was seen

The cast of *Modern Family* poses at the Screen Actors Guild Awards in January 2014. Hart had a recurring role on the show.

by a largely black audience, the MTV show drew a diverse, mainstream audience. Hart's performance was seen by more than six million viewers, which put him in the company of previous hosts, such as Chris Rock, Eddie Murphy, and Jimmy Fallon. When asked about how he planned to host the show, Hart joked, "I want to basically set myself apart from the pack," Hart said to Arati Patel from *The Hollywood Reporter*. "How do I make this event mine? How do I make this event talked about for years to come? The only way to do that is to offend people … That's what people remember." To kick off his hosting gig, Hart teamed up with celebrity couple Kanye West and Kim Kardashian to film a short promo video in which he tags along in their high-profile relationship, suggesting they nickname the group Kev-Ye-Kim.

## Let Me Explain Tour

In 2012, Hart went back on the road to stay connected to the stand-up comedy that had made his acting career possible. In his new comedy tour, Let Me Explain, Hart celebrated what he had been able to achieve from a troubled life and tackled the rumors surrounding his divorce and the struggles in his personal life. Let Me Explain took Hart to ninety American cities and even included some European and African shows. Let Me Explain sold five times as many tickets as Laugh at My Pain, including two

KEVIN HART

sold-out shows at New York City's Madison Square Garden. Hart filmed his live performance at Madison Square Garden and released it as a theatrical movie in 2013. Movie critic Roger Ebert described Hart in his review: "Prowling the stage, Hart uses his stature

Hart speaks at CinemaCon, the official convention for the National Association of Theater Owners, in 2013 to promote his comedy film *Let Me Explain*.

for maximum comic effect (he's 5'2"). His physicality is his biggest asset. As he throws himself around the stage with reckless abandon … He talks fast, and has an underlying honesty that can be very effective." *Let Me Explain* grossed $32.3 million worldwide. According to Box Office Mojo, that made it the fourth-highest-grossing stand-up comedy film of all time and proved that the unbelievable success of *Laugh at My Pain* was no fluke.

## Real Husbands of Hollywood

Based on several popular skits that aired during the 2011 BET Awards show, the *Real Husbands of Hollywood* debuted on BET in 2013. The television series was cocreated by Hart, who also starred in the mock reality show. The show followed the daily lives of Hart and other celebrities in Hollywood, including Boris Kodjoe, Nelly, Duane Martin, J. B. Smoove, Nick Cannon, and Robin Thicke, as they played fictionalized versions of themselves. The mock reality show was designed to be a parody of the popular *Real Housewives* franchise from the Bravo network. In an interview with BET, Hart explained why he wanted to be involved in the show:

> We're mocking what everybody makes fun of on a regular basis. It's ridiculous. They're fighting. They're going back and forth. We're

putting a group of men together that are talented enough and aren't afraid to make fun of themselves. We're catty. We're not getting along. We're getting along. We're friends. We're not friends, but we're doing it in a fun way. It's unique. It hasn't been done, which means it will be big.

The show premiered in January 2013 to more than four million viewers, making it BET's

At the 2014 NAACP Image Awards, Hart and fellow cast members accept the award for Outstanding Comedy Series for *Real Husbands of Hollywood*.

second-biggest network premiere. Audiences loved it, and critics gave the show positive reviews. Robert Lloyd of the *Los Angeles Times* wrote that the show's "greatest charm is in showing people who really do seem to be friends hanging out and making fun of one another and themselves. It is at its best when they all seem to be talking over one another ... which lets the viewer feel in on the joke and present at the party." The show had a successful run on BET and was renewed for five seasons, running through 2016. In 2014 and 2015, the show was nominated for several Image Awards from the NAACP (National Association for the Advancement of Colored People), winning 2014's Outstanding Comedy Series and 2014's Outstanding Actor in a Comedy Series for Hart. Finally, he had found success on the small screen.

# CHAPTER SIX

# Hollywood Superstar

By the end of 2013, Hart was an established star in Hollywood. In the past, he had been labeled as an urban comedian, appealing mainly to a black audience. Beginning in the 2010s, however, fans and Hollywood executives were beginning to see him as something else: a mainstream Hollywood superstar. He was capable of entertaining everyone—regardless of race—and his comedy, both in stand-up and scripted roles, brought in countless crowds of adoring fans.

## Playing the Leading Man

In his early films, Hart often stole scenes in smaller, supporting roles. Now, he was poised to take the next step and take on a true leading man role. In an interview with *Complex's* Justin Monroe, he said:

> I'm close. I've done a great job at being universal in my stand-up … These movies

I have coming out … are putting me in a position to become universal on an even bigger scale … If they perform how I think they will, there's astronomical potential, to where I'm not just a "black star" or a guy who some people know but a guy who everybody loves, thinks is funny, and relates to. That's the goal.

In 2014, several major films starring Hart were released. One of the biggest was *Ride Along*, a reluctant buddy cop film with costar Ice Cube. In the film, Hart plays the role of Ben Barber, a security guard who must prove to his girlfriend's brother, James Payton (Ice Cube), that he is worthy of marrying her. James, a police officer, takes Ben on a ride along to prove his toughness. Although the film received some negative reviews from critics, audiences flocked to see it. The film grossed $41 million during its opening weekend and grossed an impressive $154 million worldwide. It was also nominated for several awards, including a 2014 BET Award for Best Actor (for Hart) and two 2014 MTV Movie Award Nominations—one for Best On-Screen Duo and another for Best Comedic Performance (again for Hart). The film was also nominated for several Teen Choice Awards, with Hart winning Choice Movie Actor: Comedy. The film's success led

KEVIN HART

In the hit film *Ride Along*, Hart attempts to impress his girlfriend's brother, played by actor Ice Cube, by accompanying him in a day of his life as a police officer.

to a sequel, *Ride Along 2* (2016), with Hart and Ice Cube reprising their roles.

Also released in 2014, the romantic comedy *About Last Night* starred Hart as Bernie, who—along with costars Michael Ealy, Joy Bryant, and Regina Hall—navigates love and commitment in Los Angeles. The film was a remake of a 1986 film of the same name, this time with an all-black cast. Hart received mainly positive reviews for his performance. *New York Times* film critic A. O. Scott wrote "many of the funniest parts seem to arise spontaneously from Mr. Hart's uncensored brain and fast-moving mouth. He can swerve from tears to mock outrage to anatomically detailed obscenities faster than just about any other comic performer working today." On an estimated budget of $12.5 million, the film successfully grossed $48.6 million domestically.

In yet another 2014 hit, Hart reprised his role of Cedric in *Think Like a Man Too*. The film grossed more than $70 million worldwide. A smaller movie, *Top Five*, was also released in 2014, and though it did not break the bank for Hart, financially, it gave him an opportunity to work with one of his comedic role models: Chris Rock.

In 2015, Hart teamed up with comedian Will Farrell in a crime-based comedy titled *Get Hard*. In the film, Hart played the role of Darnell Lewis, who helps millionaire James King (Farrell) prepare to go behind bars after being arrested for fraud. Although overall reviews of the film were mixed, it was a box office success and grossed more than $111 million worldwide.

## Everyone Wants a Star

As a sign of Hart's stardom, new opportunities and accolades appeared. In 2015, Hart was asked to host *Saturday Night Live*. Years after being rejected

**KEVIN HART**

In 2015, Hart hosted an episode of the iconic television show *Saturday Night Live*, a sign of his tremendous popularity as an entertainer.

by the show, Hart was in the *SNL* offices with writers and other cast members, working on the episode in which he would be the guest star. For his opening monologue—a tradition for *SNL* hosts—Hart shared the story of his failed *SNL* audition. Working on the show that week made Hart a firm believer that everything happens for a reason. If he had been offered a job as a cast member years ago, he might not have been able to grow as a comedian and experience the success that he had today. Additionally, in 2015, Hart hosted the *Comedy Central Roast of Justin Bieber*. The *Comedy Central Roast* is a series of specials where a group of celebrities are invited to make fun of (or roast) the subject of the show and the other guests as well.

At the 2015 MTV Movie Awards, Hart's comedic talent was recognized. He was awarded the second-ever Comedic Genius Award. The first Comedic Genius Award went to Will Farrell, Hart's costar in *Get Hard*. According to MTV, the award recognized Hart's "bold and irreverent comedic style that has captivated audiences from his movies and sitcoms, to stand-up specials, award show performances and in front of packed arenas of fans." To accept the award, Hart brought his two kids—Heaven and Hendrix—on stage. In his acceptance speech, Hart put the jokes aside and thanked the people who had helped him reach the top of his field. Particularly, he paid respect to his children and his fans. Though his career has erupted with more success than he could have ever imagined, he has remained humble and thankful for the people in his life.

To continue his very special 2015, Hart was selected as one of *TIME* magazine's 100 most influential men and women in the world.

# HELP FROM THE HART

In 2018, Hart joined with UNCF (United Negro College Fund) and KIPP (Knowledge is Power Program) to launch a new UNCF scholarship program. Through his Help from the Hart Charity, Hart established a $600,000 scholarship program that will provide eighteen college scholarships for KIPP students who are attending eleven historically black colleges and universities.

Though college was not a good fit for Hart, he recognizes the importance of a good education, especially for black youths in the United States. He is

Hart supports the UNCF (United Negro College Fund) headed by Dr. Michael Lomax, pictured here. Hart donates to UNCF to fund college scholarships for black youth in the United States.

# Hollywood Superstar

> very well aware that making it—as he has—in show business is very difficult and very rare, so he wants to give other people a chance to succeed in more conventional occupations.

Appearing on the list was an honor, shared with other world leaders, artists, and influencers. In a tribute to Hart published in *TIME* magazine, Chris Rock wrote:

> After he makes you laugh for an hour, you feel like you're his friend—you feel his joy and his pain … That makes him a new kind of cool … In Kevin's comedy, there's the minute observations of Jerry Seinfeld, the family-oriented storytelling of Bill Cosby and the open-wound honesty of Richard Pryor. But mostly there's a lot of Kevin Hart.

## A Second Chance at Love

In his personal life, Hart had found a new love in aspiring model and actress Eniko Parrish. After meeting in 2009, the couple began dating shortly after Hart separated from his wife Torrei. Over the years, the couple dated steadily, and Parrish frequently accompanied Hart to his shows and events. In 2014, Hart proposed to Parrish on her thirtieth birthday in front of friends and family. Hart admits that the decision to get married again—after his first marriage ended in divorce—was difficult. Two years later, however, Hart and Parrish married in a romantic ceremony in Santa Barbara, California. Hart's son Hendrix served as his father's best man.

In October 2016, a few months into the new marriage, Hart talked about his happiness with married life:

> You get to laugh every day. For no reason at all. You just laugh. I'm a very pleasant person to be around; it's very rare to see me on a bad day … I pride myself on living, loving and laughing. I spread that energy wherever I am, with whomever can be touched. My spirit is contagious and my wife gets it firsthand.

In 2017, however, Hart's marriage hit a bump when he admitted to cheating on his wife. In an October Instagram post, Hart told fans about an extortion attempt that included a video of him and another woman. At the time, Parrish was eight months pregnant with Hart's third child. "I'm guilty, regardless of how it happened and what was involved … I'm guilty. I'm wrong," Hart admitted in a radio interview on Power 105.1 FM. "It's beyond irresponsible. There's no way around

Hollywood Superstar

After his divorce, Hart began dating model and actress Eniko Parrish. The couple married in 2016 and had a son together, Kenzo Hart, in 2017.

it. That's Kevin Hart in his dumbest moment. That's not the finest hour of my life."

In November 2017, Parrish gave birth to a baby boy, Kenzo. After his open apology, Hart and Parrish have worked to rebuild their marriage. According to Hart, he is grateful that Parrish has chosen to forgive him. "I applaud my wife for just displaying a high level of strength that I can't even explain," Hart told Janine Rubenstein of *People* magazine. "I applaud her for being my backbone, my support system, and more importantly, taking my life to the next level." In August 2018, the couple celebrated their two-year anniversary. Hart says he cannot imagine his life without Parrish. "The money, the entertainment, the movies, it's great, those are blessings, but the level that I've reached from a happy standpoint, that woman is 100% responsible for it," he told *People*.

# CHAPTER SEVEN

# *I Can't Make This Up*

Riding the wave of his recent successes, Hart returned again to his first love: stand-up comedy. In 2015, he launched his What Now? comedy tour, which became one of the highest-grossing comedy tours of all time. It sold more than one million tickets and grossed more than $100 million. In shows on five continents and fifteen countries, Hart wowed audiences with his high-energy show that incorporated an elaborate set with video screens, fire columns, and other props and effects. In New York City, Hart sold out two shows at Madison Square Garden, one at the Barclays Center in Brooklyn, and another at the Prudential Center in Newark, New Jersey. "The tour is truly remarkable," Geof Wills—president of Live Nation Comedy—told Ray Waddell of Billboard.com. He noted that What Now?'s

Shown here, Hart attends a screening of his new comedy film, *Kevin Hart: What Now?*, in his hometown of Philadelphia in 2016.

average ticket price was a whopping $70 and ticket demand supported multiple shows in an area—often two sellouts in one night. While other comedians might focus on television or movies, Wills said that Hart "wants to do the films, the specials *and* the concerts. Kevin is really going for it all."

Hart ended the tour at Lincoln Financial Field in his hometown of Philadelphia, making him the first comedian to headline a National Football League stadium. The show—performed before an audience of about fifty-three thousand people—was filmed and released in theaters in 2016 as *Kevin Hart: What Now?* In a film review for the *Washington Post*, Pat Padua wrote:

> The movie's pleasures lie in its simplest element: Hart's storytelling. Creating vivid characters along the way, Hart uses his whole body to sell a joke. His expressive face gets his biggest laughs with a recurring joke about black women who don't believe anything you say…Despite the free association, Hart has fine-tuned his routine for the most efficient structure and timing.

The film generated nearly $24 million at the box office, making it the fifth-highest-grossing stand-up comedy film of all time, according to Box Office Mojo.

## Keeping It Universal

Part of Hart's universal appeal is the fact that he shies away from controversy in his shows. He refuses to make political jokes. Political jokes have long been a core component in comedy—both onstage and on-screen—because nearly everyone has strong reactions to politics, whether positive or negative. Hart, however, does not want to make jokes about the political issues in the twenty-first century world.

Instead, Hart believes that his job as a comedian is to spread a positive message and make people laugh—not focus their attention on something that makes them mad. He told Matt Wilstein of The Daily Beast:

> I want to be a bright spot. I want to take your mind off of whatever may be going on in your life that could be wrong and give you a reason to say, you know what? It's going to be OK. That's being the positive, motivating, inspiring person that I am, that I always will be.

Hart sees political topics as something that divides people. There are so many other, less controversial topics that can generate big laughs, and those are the subjects Hart targets when he writes new material.

In addition to his comedy tours, Hart has continued to be a bankable star at the box office. Between 2016 and 2018, he appeared in several movies. In 2016, he starred in the action comedy *Central Intelligence* with Dwayne "the Rock" Johnson. The film follows two high school classmates who reconnect via Facebook and become involved in the world of

*I Can't Make This Up*

international espionage. A box office success, *Central Intelligence* grossed $217 million worldwide. Also in 2016, Hart starred in the sequel *Ride Along 2*, a film that generated more than $120 million. In 2017, Hart starred in *Jumanji: Welcome to the Jungle*. The film is a reboot of the 1995 film *Jumanji*, which starred the late comedian Robin Williams. It was a smashing success, generating $404 million in the United States and $962 million worldwide.

In 2018, Hart starred with rising comedic star and longtime friend Tiffany Haddish in *Night School*. The film was a success at the box office, proving Hart's appeal as a comedic leading man.

In 2018, Hart starred in—and coproduced—*Night School*, a comedy about a group of adults who are trying to earn their GEDs. The film also stars rising comedian Tiffany Haddish, who has long been a friend to Hart. For the first time, Hart was also credited with being one of the cowriters of the film script. The film received mixed reviews from critics, despite its star-studded cast. "Hart grabs a few giggles when his character takes a job at a joint called Christian Chicken, and Haddish adds a dab of physical comedy when she beats up Teddy in a training session. But hardly anything in this movie makes sense," wrote Peter Travers for *Rolling Stone*. Though the critical reviews were mixed, the film was successful, grossing $74 million within six weeks of its release on September 28, 2018.

During this time, Hart also ventured into animated films, providing the voice of the bad rabbit, Snowball, in *The Secret Life of Pets* in 2016. The film was yet another box office hit, grossing more than $800 million worldwide and becoming the highest-grossing animated film not produced by either Disney or Pixar. A sequel, *The Secret Life of Pets 2*, is already being planned. Hart also provided the voice of George Beard in the 2017 action comedy *Captain Underpants*, an animated film based on Dav Pilkey's popular children's book series of the same name.

## Taking It to the Bank

Years of hard work have paid off financially for Hart. In 2015, *Forbes* magazine named him the second-highest-paid comedian. Between his movie and television appearances and the What Now? tour, Hart earned $28.5 million, putting him behind only the legendary comedian Jerry Seinfeld, whose career has spanned decades.

In 2016, Hart played more than one hundred shows worldwide and appeared in both movies and television. Because of this enormous workload, Hart jumped to the top of the earnings list, with a reported income of $87.5 million, much of which came from his massively popular tour appearances. He became the first comedian ever to earn more than Seinfeld. His earnings also catapulted him to number six on the list of highest-paid celebrities in 2016, which placed him above many actors, musicians, and athletes. In 2017, Hart earned an estimated $32.5 million. While he did not make the top of the list that year, he has found a better balance between work and family life.

## Adding Author to His Résumé

In addition to his work on stage and screen, Hart published his memoir in 2017: *I Can't Make This Up: Life Lessons*. In the book, Hart goes into detail about his life growing up in Philadelphia, his family

# KEVIN HART

life with a drug-addicted dad, and the challenges he faced professionally and personally on his rise to fame. As fans of his stand-up already knew, he was not afraid of baring his soul in a public forum. Accordingly, his memoir describes his sometimes challenging, but eventually successful, climb to the top.

Hart has said that he wrote the book to motivate others and show them that a person can face challenges and still find success.

*After rising to the top of the entertainment world, Hart released* I Can't Make This Up: Life Lessons *in 2017.*

On June 25, 2017, Hart's memoir was number one on the *New York Times* bestseller list for print and e-book nonfiction. A starred review from *Publisher's Weekly* praised the book: "Comedian Hart tells all in this emotion-filled memoir full of grit and humor … Like Hart's standup, the book's tone is self-deprecating and honest … Inspiring and thoroughly entertaining, Hart's memoir brings his readers into his hilarious universe of stories and philosophy."

## Business Mogul

More than just an entertainer, Hart has also established himself as a savvy businessman. His company HartBeat Productions has produced three successful stand-up specials. In 2017, he launched the Laugh Out Loud (LOL) Network in partnership with Lionsgate, a major production studio. LOL is a streaming service that delivers original and unscripted comedy series, licensed programming, stand-up specials, and live broadcasts. The programming includes shows like *Cold as Balls*—in which Hart interviews sports celebrities in an ice bath—and *Kevin Hart: What the Fit*, in which Hart tries playing obscure sports with celebrities.

The idea of forming a digital content service developed as a way to leverage Hart's growing global popularity. Because of his enormous fame and universal appeal, people all over the world—especially young audiences—are always hungry for more Hart-related content. Because so many people have smartphones—again, particularly younger people—it made complete sense to create the LOL Network to connect with people on their mobile devices.

At the end of 2017, HartBeat Productions announced that it had signed a two-year, first-look deal with Universal Studios, which had produced many of Hart's previous movies. The deal gives

KEVIN HART

## PITCHING PRODUCTS

With Hart's popularity, companies are always knocking on his door to sign him up as a pitchman for their products. Even with so much demand, Hart remains selective about what products he is willing to endorse. He prefers to work with only a limited number of brands that he believes in, wears, or uses himself. Some of those brands include Nike, Mountain Dew, and underwear company Tommy John. In 2018, Hart launched a new campaign with Mountain Dew Kickstart that features a video series called "Courtside Do's and Don'ts with Kevin Hart," which shows off Hart's self-deprecating humor and physical comedy on the NBA sidelines. A huge NBA fan, Hart says the partnership with Mountain Dew fits well into his personal brand. In the same way, Hart not only stars in Tommy John campaigns, he also designs and wears the brand's underwear and has invested in the company.

Universal the first chance to acquire any of HartBeat's creative projects. For example, Hart's 2018 film *Night School* was the first major movie in the HartBeat portfolio.

HartBeat Productions also has a number of projects in development that do not star Hart.

This is all part of his long-term plan to create a sustainable business that is independent of him as an entertainer. The world of show business is notoriously fickle; crowds can go from loving an entertainer to hating him or her very quickly. Even if Hart does fall out of favor, however, his company and his business interests will still be going strong. He is building a strong base with which to protect the future for his family.

## No Limits

In October 2017, Hart announced that he was going back on the road. On The Irresponsible Tour, the comedian performed in cities across North America as well as Europe, Australia, and Asia throughout 2018. Hart announced the tour in a goofy, profane video trailer in which five versions of Hart—the author, athlete, mogul, actor, and comic—argue with each other.

   Looking toward his very bright future, Hart believes that there is nothing he cannot achieve. He has already raised himself from a small-time Philadelphia comic to the top comedian in the world—and maybe the greatest comedic entertainer of all time. Though he faces stiff competition for that throne, his diversity—as a stand-up performer, actor, producer, writer, and more—and the sheer amount of content he works on continue to make his case stronger every year.

# Fact Sheet on Kevin Hart

**Full name:** Kevin Darnell Hart
**Birthplace:** Philadelphia, Pennsylvania
**Birthdate:** July 6, 1979
**Parents:** Nancy Hart and Henry Witherspoon
**High School:** George Washington High School in Philadelphia, Pennsylvania
**College attended:** Community College of Philadelphia (did not graduate)
**Marital status:** Married to Torrei Hart (2003–2011) and Eniko Parrish (2016–present)
**Children:** Heaven Leigh Hart (born 2005), Hendrix Kevin Hart (born 2007), and Kenzo Hart (born 2017)
**Height:** 5 feet 4 inches (1.62 m) tall
**First public appearance:** The Laff House in Philadelphia, Pennsylvania
**Comedic influences:** Chris Rock, Eddie Murphy, Bill Cosby, George Carlin, and Jerry Seinfeld
**Career if he wasn't a comedian:** Shoe salesman or hand model
**Dream movie costar:** Denzel Washington
**Favorite book:** *Of Mice and Men,* by John Steinbeck
**Biggest phobia:** Reptiles
**Biggest regret:** Not giving 110 percent in school
**Favorite sport:** Basketball

# Fact Sheet on Kevin Hart's Work

## Comedy Specials and Films
**2008** *I'm a Grown Little Man*
**2010** *Seriously Funny*
**2011** *Laugh at My Pain*
**2013** *Let Me Explain*
**2016** *What Now?*

## Television Credits
**2001** *North Hollywood*, Kevin Heart
**2002** *Class of '06*, Tony
**2002–2003** *Undeclared*, Luke
**2004** *The Big House*, Kevin
**2005** *Barbershop*, James Ricky
**2005** *Dante*
**2005–2006** *Jake in Progress*, Nugget Dawson
**2006** *Help Me Help You*, Kevin
**2006** *Love, Inc.,* James
**2007** *All of Us*, Greg
**2007** *The Weekend*, Miles
**2009** *Kröd Mändoon and the Flaming Sword of Fire*, Zezelryck
**2009** *Party Down*, Dro Grizzle
**2010** *Cubed*, Security guard
**2011** *Little in Common*, Ty Burleson
**2011–2012** *Modern Family*, Andre
**2014** *College Humor Originals*, himself
**2014** *Keep It Together*

# KEVIN HART

2016 *Clevver Now*, himself
2017 *Kevin Hart Presents: The Next Level*, host
2018 *TKO: Total Knock Out*

## Film Credits
2002 *Paper Soldiers*, Shawn
2003 *Death of a Dynasty*, P-Diddy/cop 1/dance coach
2003 *Scary Movie 3*, CJ
2004 *Along Came Polly*, Vic
2004 *Soul Plane*, Nashawn
2005 *In the Mix*, Busta
2005 *The 40-Year-Old Virgin*, smart tech customer
2006 *Scary Movie 4*, CJ
2006 *The Last Stand*, F Stop/G Spot
2007 *Epic Movie*, Silas (uncredited)
2008 *Drillbit Taylor*, pawn shop employee
2008 *Extreme Movie*, Barry
2008 *Fool's Gold*, Bigg Bunny
2008 *Meet Dave*, No. 17
2008 *Superhero Movie*, Trey
2009 *Not Easily Broken*, Tree
2010 *Death at a Funeral*, Brian
2010 *Little Fockers,* Nurse Louis
2010 *Something Like a Business*, JoJo
2011 *35 and Ticking*, Cleavon
2011 *Let Go*, Kris
2012 *Exit Strategy*, mannequin head man

**2012** *The Five-Year Engagement*, Doug
**2012** *Think Like a Man*, Cedric
**2013** *Grudge Match*, Dante Slate, Jr.
**2013** *This Is the End*, Kevin Hart
**2014** *About Last Night*, Bernie
**2014** *Ride Along*, Ben Barber
**2014** *Think Like a Man Too*, Cedric
**2014** *Top Five*, Charles
**2015** *Get Hard*, Darnell
**2015** *The Wedding Ringer*, Jimmy Callahan/Bic
**2016** *Central Intelligence*, Calvin Joyner
**2016** *Ride Along 2*, Ben Barber
**2016** *The Secret Life of Pets,* Snowball (voice)
**2017** *Captain Underpants: The First Epic Movie*, George (voice)
**2017** *Jumanji: Welcome to the Jungle*, Fridge
**2017** *The Upside*, Dell
**2018** *Night School*, Teddy Walker

# Books
**2017** *I Can't Make This Up: Life Lessons*, published by Atria/37 INK

# Awards
**2012** BET Award for Best Actor in *Kevin Hart: Laugh at My Pain*
**2014** NAACP Image Award for Outstanding Comedy Series, *Real Husbands of Hollywood*

**2014** NAACP Image Award for Outstanding Actor in a Comedy Series, *Real Husbands of Hollywood*

**2014** NAACP Image Award for Entertainer of the Year

**2014** Nickelodeon Kids' Choice Award, Favorite Funny Star

**2014** Teen Choice Award, Choice Movie Actor: Comedy, *Ride Along*

**2014** Teen Choice Award, Choice Comedian

**2015** MTV Movie Award, Comedic Genius Award

**2016** Billboard Touring Award, Top Comedy Tour

**2016** People's Choice Awards, Favorite Comedic Movie Actor, *The Wedding Ringer*

**2016** People's Choice Awards, Favorite Cable TV Actor, *Real Husbands of Hollywood*

**2017** People's Choice Awards, Favorite Comedic Movie Actor, *Central Intelligence*

**2017** Nickelodeon Kids' Choice Awards, Favorite Villain and Most Wanted Pet, *The Secret Life of Pets*

**2017** Nickelodeon Kids' Choice Awards, Best Friends Forever (shared with Dwayne Johnson), *Central Intelligence*

# Critical Reviews

### What Now?
"Hart is more consistently on-target than in any of his prior concerts. Assisted by several giant screens onstage, Hart works the audience over visually and verbally … 'Kevin Hart: What Now?' is Kevin Hart at the top of his game."—Odie Henderson, RogerEbert.com

### Laugh at My Pain
"Comedian Kevin Hart's hybrid standup film *Laugh at My Pain* is at its best when it takes that title to heart. Riding a deserved wave of popularity on the comedy circuit, Hart can unveil a sex gag with the best of them, but it's his gimlet-eyed take on his own rather unfunny troubles—a drug-addict father, a recently deceased mother, a divorce—that mark him as a funnyman worthy of attention."—Andrew Barker, *Variety*

### Let Me Explain
"Diminutive and energetic, he exudes comedy with every spirited step and elaborate gesture. He's hilarious, but almost as important, he's self-aware enough to joke about his own shortcomings, which makes appreciating *Let Me Explain* so much easier."—Stephanie Merry, *Washington Post*

### Ride Along
"If you're a fan of pint-size motormouth Kevin Hart's stand-up comedy, you're likely to have fun with this. Just don't go looking for a motion picture with credible characters or an overly involving story."—Glenn Kenny, RogerEbert.com

### The Big House
"Hart ... [as] a stand-up comic, is an engaging presence who uses his 5-foot-4 stature to his advantage: He is cute no matter what he does."—Robert Lloyd, *Los Angeles Times*

### I Can't Make This Up: Life Lessons
"Indeed, Kevin Hart's life story is very fascinating. Readers will feel like they are in the scenes with him in his trials and joys alike and gain valuable lessons for their lives."—Pat Cuadros, Blogcritics.org

# Timeline

**1979** Kevin Hart is born on July 6 in Philadelphia, Pennsylvania.

**1997** Hart graduates from George Washington High School in Philadelphia.

**2001** Hart films the *North Hollywood* television pilot, but it is cancelled before airing on television.

**2002** Hart stars in the film *Paper Soldiers*.

**2003** Hart marries Torrei Hart.

**2004** Hart develops a short-lived television show, *The Big House*, which runs for six episodes on the ABC Network. He stars in another movie, *Soul Plane*.

**2005** Hart's daughter, Heaven Leigh Hart, is born in March.

**2007** Hart's mother, Nancy Hart, passes away from cancer. Hart's son Hendrix Kevin Hart is born in November.

**2009** Hart releases his first comedy album, *I'm a Grown Little Man*. He forms a production company, HartBeat Productions.

**2010** Hart releases his second comedy special: *Seriously Funny*.

**2011** Kevin and Torrei Hart divorce. His production company releases *Laugh at My Pain* comedy film. He hosts the BET Awards show.

**2012** Hart hosts the MTV Video Music Awards. He receives the BET Award for Best Actor in *Laugh* *at My Pain*. He stars in *Think Like a Man*. He launches a new stand-up tour, Let Me Explain.

**2013** The *Let Me Explain* stand-up movie is released. *The Real Husbands of Hollywood* debuts.

**2014** Hart receives several awards, including the Teen Choice Award for Choice Movie Actor and the NAACP Image Award for Entertainer of the Year. He stars with Ice Cube in *Ride Along*.

**2015** Hart receives the MTV Comedic Genius Award. He becomes the second-highest-paid comedian in the world. He hosts *Saturday Night Live*. He is selected as one of *TIME* magazine's 100 Most Influential People of the Year.

**2016** Hart marries longtime girlfriend Eniko Parrish. He releases his fourth comedy album, *What Now?*; he appears with Dwayne Johnson in *Central Intelligence*. Hart receives a star on the Hollywood Walk of Fame.

**2017** Hart publishes his memoir, *I Can't Make This Up: Life Lessons*. He launches the streaming comedy service Laugh Out Loud Network in partnership with Lionsgate. He admits to cheating on Parrish. His son Kenzo Kash Hart is born in November.

**2018** Hart embarks on his Irresponsible worldwide comedy tour.

# Glossary

**amateur**  A person who engages in a pursuit on an unpaid basis.
**anecdote**  A narration of a humorous and interesting event.
**blockbuster**  A movie that is a great commercial success.
**commission**  An amount of money, usually a percentage, paid to a salesperson.
**diligent**  Showing care in one's duties or work.
**endorse**  To recommend a product in an advertisement.
**ensemble**  A group of actors who perform together.
**espionage**  The practice of spying or using spies.
**eviction**  The act of kicking someone out, such as a tenant from a property.
**extortion**  Obtaining money through the use of force or threats.
**headline**  To appear as the star performer at a concert or show.
**improvise**  To create or perform something without preparation.
**incentive**  Something that motivates or encourages someone.
**leverage**  To influence a person or situation to achieve a desired outcome.
**memoir**  An autobiography.
**memorabilia**  Objects collected that are associated with a specific person or event.

**mimic** To imitate another person to entertain others.

**niche** A comfortable position in life or employment.

**nuance** A subtle difference in meaning.

**persona** A character played by an actor or entertainer.

**pilot** A television show made to test the audience reaction and viability as a series.

**premiere** The first showing of a movie or television show.

**profane** Using offensive language or content.

**reality show** A television program in which real people are filmed in their daily lives or in predetermined situations.

**revelation** Something that was previously unknown.

**sequel** A movie, book, or other work that continues after an earlier work.

**skits** Short comedy performances.

**stage name** A fake name used by an actor or entertainer.

**sustainable** Able to be maintained at a certain level over time.

**theatrics** Staged effects during a performance.

**trajectory** The path followed by an object.

**turmoil** A state of confusion, uncertainty, or disturbance.

**universal** Applicable to all people or things in a given category.

# For More Information

Academy of Motion Picture Arts and Sciences
8949 Wilshire Boulevard
Beverly Hills, CA 90211
(310) 247-3000
Website: http://www.oscars.org
Facebook, Twitter, and Instagram: @TheAcademy
The Academy of Motion Picture Arts and Sciences is one of the world's leading movie-related organizations and represents thousands of men and women working in cinema.

BET Networks
1540 Broadway
New York, NY 10036
Website: http://www.bet.com
Facebook, Twitter, and Instagram: @BET
Black Entertainment Television (BET) is an American pay television channel that targets African American audiences and is owned by the BET Networks, a division of Viacom.

Canadian Association of Stand-Up Comedians
1330 Gerrard Street East
Toronto ON M4L 1Y7
Canada
Website: https://canadianstandup.ca
Facebook, Twitter, and Instagram: @canadianstandup
The association was formed in 2017 with the goal of increasing opportunities for stand-up comics in Canada.

The Internet & Television Association
25 Massachusetts Avenue NW, #100
Washington, DC 20001
Website: http://www.ncta.com
Twitter: @NCTAitv
The Internet & Television Association is the principal trade association for the US broadband and pay television industries. It represents more than 90 percent of the US cable market.

Just for Laughs
2101 St. Laurent Boulevard
Montreal QC 2T5 H2X
Canada
(514) 845-3155
Website: http://www.justforlaughs.com
Facebook, Twitter, and Instagram: @justforlaughs
Just for Laughs is a comedy festival held every year in Montreal, Canada, and it attracts some of the biggest names in show business—including Kevin Hart.

Motion Picture Association of America
1301 K Street NW, Suite 900E
Washington, DC 2005
(202) 293-1966
Website: http://www.mpaa.org
Facebook: @MotionPictureAssociationAmerica

## For More Information

Instagram: @motionpictureassociation
Twitter: @MPAA
The Motion Picture Association of America is a trade association representing the major film studios of Hollywood.

# For Further Reading

Aldridge, Rebecca. *Stephen Colbert*. New York, NY: Rosen Publishing, 2016.

Apatow, Judd. *Sick in the Head: Conversations about Life and Comedy*. New York, NY: Random House, 2015.

Friedman, Budd. *The Improv: An Oral History of the Comedy Club That Revolutionized Stand-Up*. Dallas, TX: BenBella Books, 2017.

Haddish, Tiffany. *The Last Black Unicorn*. New York, NY: Gallery Books, 2017.

Harrison, Kathryn. *Tina Fey*. New York, NY: Rosen Publishing, 2016.

Hart, Kevin. *I Can't Make This Up: Life Lessons*. New York, NY: Atria/37 Ink, 2017.

Hill, Z. B. *Comedy & Comedians*. Broomall, PA: Mason Crest, 2014.

Kaplan, Arie. *Saturday Night Live: Shaping TV Comedy and American Culture*. Minneapolis, MN: Twenty-First Century Books, 2014.

Kauffman, Susan. *Kevin Hart: Comedian, Actor, Writer, and Producer*. New York, NY: Enslow, 2018.

Klein, Rebecca. *Jimmy Fallon*. New York, NY: Rosen Publishing, 2016.

Krumsiek, Allison. *Stephen Colbert: Late-Night Comedy Leader*. Farmington Hills, MI: Lucent Books, 2018.

Marcovitz, Hal. *Eddie Murphy: Actor*. Langhorne, PA: Chelsea House, 2011.

# For Further Reading

Nagelhout, Ryan. *Dwayne Johnson: The Rock's Rise to Fame*. Farmington Hills, MI: Lucent Books, 2018.

Nagle, Jeanne. *Chris Rock*. New York, NY: Rosen Publishing, 2016.

Niver, Heather Moore. *Aziz Ansari*. New York, NY: Rosen Publishing, 2016.

Noah, Trevor. *Born a Crime: Stories from a South African Childhood*. New York, NY: Spiegel & Grau, 2016.

Rosenfield, Stephen. *Mastering Stand-Up*. Chicago, IL: Chicago Review Press, 2018.

Schuman, Michael. *Margaret Cho: Comedian, Actress, and Activist*. New York, NY: Enslow, 2016.

Seinfeld, Jerry. *SeinLanguage*. New York, NY: Bantam Books, 2008.

Shofner, Melissa Raae. *Tina Fey: Queen of Comedy*. Farmington Hills, MI: Lucent Books, 2017.

Shoup, Kate. *Ellen DeGeneres: Television Comedian and Gay Rights Activist*. New York, NY: Cavendish Square, 2016.

Todd, Anne. *Chris Rock: Comedian and Actor*. Langhorne, PA: Chelsea House, 2006.

Uschan, Michael. *Tyler Perry*. Farmington Hills, MI: Lucent Books, 2010.

Wasson, Sam. *Improv Nation: How We Made a Great American Art*. New York, NY: Houghton Mifflin Harcourt, 2017.

Whitaker, Mark. *Cosby: His Life and Times*. New York, NY: Simon & Schuster, 2014.

# Bibliography

ABC7.com Staff. "Kevin Hart honored with star on Hollywood Walk of Fame." ABC7.com, October 10, 2016. https://abc7.com/entertainment/kevin-hart-honored-with-star-on-hollywood-walk-of-fame/1549079.

Blair, Iain. "Walk of Fame Honoree Kevin Hart is Non-Stop." *Variety*, October 10, 2016. https://variety.com/2016/film/awards/walk-of-fame-honoree-kevin-hart-1201876409.

Crump, Ahmaad. "Kevin Hart to Host BET Awards, Star in New Film." WZAK Cleveland. Retrieved November 20, 2018. https://wzakcleveland.com/2816721/kevin-hart-to-host-bet-awards-star-in-new-film.

Frieswick, Kris. "How Kevin Hart Went From Being a Comedian to the Guy Who Owns Comedy." *Entrepreneur*, May 22, 2018. https://www.entrepreneur.com/article/313228.

Gettell, Oliver. "Kevin Hart to Receive Comedic Genius honor at MTV Movie Awards," *Los Angeles Times*, March 31, 2015. http://www.latimes.com/entertainment/movies/moviesnow/la-et-mn-kevin-hart-to-receive-comedic-genius-honor-at-mtv-movie-awards-20150331-story.html.

Hart, Kevin. *I Can't Make This Up: Life Lessons*. New York, NY: Atria/37 Ink, 2017.

Lang, Brett. "Writing His Own Story." *Variety*, May 2017. https://variety.com/2017/film/features

# Bibliography

/kevin-hart-interview-childhood-i-cant-make-this-up-1202446225.

McClurg, Jocelyn. "Kevin Hart: 'I'm an Open Book,' and New Memoir Proves It." USAToday.com, June 4, 2017. https://www.usatoday.com/story/life/books/2017/06/04/kevin-hart-i-cant-make-this-up-book-bookcon/102496130.

McNary, Dave. "Kevin Hart Partners with Lionsgate on Laugh Out Loud Streaming Service." *Variety*, March 31, 2016. https://variety.com/2016/digital/news/kevin-hart-vod-service-lionsgate-laugh-out-loud-1201742608.

Monroe, Justin. "Interview: Kevin Hart Talks Being More Than a 'Black Star,' Scary-Ass Robert De Niro, and Why He's the Modern Eddie Murphy." *Complex*, December 23, 2013. https://www.complex.com/pop-culture/2013/12/kevin-hart-grudge-match-ride-along-interview.

Padua, Pat. "'Kevin Hart: What Now?' Documents a Sold-Out Comedy Show at a Football Stadium." *Washington Post*, October 13, 2016. https://www.washingtonpost.com/goingoutguide/movies/kevin-hart-what-now-documents-a-sold-out-comedy-show-at-a-football-stadium/2016/10/13/8fe808a2-8f01-11e6-a6a3-d50061aa9fae_story.html?utm_term=.b4386c65f49a.

Patel, Arati. "MTV Video Music Awards 2012: Host Kevin Hart Takes THR on Tour of Set,

Backstage." *The Hollywood Reporter*, September 5, 2012. https://www.hollywoodreporter.com/earshot/kevin-hart-mtv-video-music-awards-stage-tour-367922.

Peoplestaff225. "Is Kevin Hart a Fun Dad or a Tough Dad? (Both, He Says!)" *People*, March 17, 2015. https://people.com/parents/kevin-hart-fun-tough-dad-get-hard-premiere.

*Publisher's Weekly*. Review of *I Can't Make This Up: Life Lessons*, by Kevin Hart. June 6, 2017. https://www.publishersweekly.com/978-1-5011-5556-7.

Rock, Chris. "Kevin Hart." *TIME*, April 16, 2015. http://time.com/collection-post/3823293/kevin-hart-2015-time-100.

Rubenstein, Janine. "Kevin Hart Reveals How Wife Eniko Forgave Him after Cheating Scandal: 'She's My Backbone.'" *People*, September 26, 2018. https://people.com/movies/kevin-hart-reveals-wife-eniko-forgave-him-after-cheating-scandal.

Scott, A. O. "With a Dentist's Chair and a Chicken Mask, a Girl Can't Say No." *New York Times*, February 13, 2014. https://www.nytimes.com/2014/02/14/movies/in-about-last-night-couples-map-differing-paths-to-love.html.

Smith, Tracy. "Kevin Hart: What's So Funny?" CBS News, May 28, 2017. https://www.cbsnews.com/news/kevin-hart-whats-so-funny.

# Bibliography

Waddell, Ray. "Kevin Hart Is on Track for the Biggest Comedy Tour of All Time." Bilboard.com, March 6, 2015. https://www.billboard.com/articles/business/6494723/kevin-hart-biggest-comedy-tour-ever-what-now.

Weiner, Jonah. "Kevin Hart's Funny Business." *Rolling Stone*, July 29, 2015. https://www.rollingstone.com/movies/movie-news/kevin-harts-funny-business-67836.

Wilstein, Matt. "Kevin Hart on Creating Tidal for Comedy and Why He Refuses to Joke About Trump." The Daily Beast, August 10, 2017. https://www.thedailybeast.com/kevin-hart-on-creating-tidal-for-comedy-and-why-he-refuses-to-joke-about-trump.

Zemler, Emily. "Comedian Kevin Hart Is Probably the Most Ambitious Man on the Planet." *Esquire*, October 13, 2016. https://www.esquire.com/entertainment/movies/q-and-a/a49564/kevin-hart-interview-what-now.

# Index

## A
*About Last Night*, 68–69
actor, 6, 40, 87
*Along Came Polly*, 41
amateur competition, 25
amateur night, 23–25
anecdotal comedy, 27–28
APA Agency, 7
Apatow, Judd, 40
auditions, 34, 38, 40, 44, 70
award nominations, 67
awards, 65, 67, 71

## B
Becky, Dave, 6, 38, 44
Berkowitz, Mike, 6–8
best-known line, 56
BET Awards Show, 52, 60, 63
*Big House, The*, 41, 42, 50
birth, 10
blended family, 6
Boston Comedy Club, 34
breaking into business, 34–43
businessman, 84–87

## C
*Captain Underpants*, 82
*Central Intelligence*, 80
childhood, 10–21
City Sports, 21, 22, 25, 26
Clanagan, Jeff, 58, 59
class clown, 16
*Cold as Balls*, 85
college, 20–21
Comedic Genius Award, 71
Comedy Central, 45, 47, 51, 56
*Comedy Central Presents*, 43
*Comedy Central Roast of Justin Bieber*, 71
*Comic View: One Mic Stand*, 52
Community College of Philadelphia, 20, 36
coparent, 53
Cosby, Bill, 73

## D
Dash, Damon, 38–40
deadpan delivery, 28
*Death at a Funeral*, 51
*Def Comedy Jam*, 29
divorce, 36, 53, 61, 74

## E
earnings, 83
education, 16

## F
Farrell, Will, 69, 71
first comedy set, 18
*Fools Gold*, 44, 49
*40-Year-Old Virgin, The*, 44
future, 87

# Index

## G
George Washington High School, 20
*Get Hard*, 69, 71
getting personal, 35, 37
gigs around town, 29
Gotham Comedy Club, 34

## H
Haddish, Tiffany, 81, 82
Hart, Heaven (daughter), 6, 36, 45, 71
Hart, Hendrix (son), 6, 36, 46, 71, 74
Hart, Kenzo (son), 74
Hart, Nancy (mother), 10, 21
  as role model, 10–12
  death of, 49
Hart, Robert Kenneth (brother), 10, 12–13, 49, 50
Hart, Torrei (ex-wife), 6, 35, 36, 45–48, 52–53, 73
HartBeat Productions, 57, 58, 85, 86
Harvey, Steve, 59
Help from the Hart Charity, 72–73
Hollywood superstar, 66–76
Hollywood Walk of Fame, 6
hometown, 6

## I
*I Can't Make This Up: Life Lessons*, 16, 83
Ice Cube, 6, 67, 68
Image Awards, 65
*I'm a Grown Little Man*, 44–53
improvisation, 39, 59
infidelity, 74
Irresponsible Tour, The, 87

## J
Johnson, Dwayne, 80
*Jumanji: Welcome to the Jungle*, 81
Just for Laughs Festival, 37–38, 50

## K
*Kevin Hart: What Now?*, 79
*Kevin Hart: What the Fit*, 85
Knowledge is Power Program (KIPP), 72

## L
Laff House, 23, 25, 26, 29, 50
*Laugh at My Pain*, 58–59, 63
Laugh at My Pain tour, 55–56, 61
Laugh Out Loud (LOL) Network, 85
leading man, 66–69

Let Me Explain tour, 61–63
life changes, 45
Lil' Kev, 22–33
*Little Fockers*, 51
Los Angeles, California, 36, 40, 43, 44, 57, 68

## M

Madison Square Garden, 61, 62, 77
marketing, 48–49
marriage (first), 36
  end of, 52–53
marriage (second), 73–74
*Meet Dave*, 44
memoir, 16, 18, 57, 83–84
*Modern Family*, 60
Montreal, Canada, 37
most influential, 71–72
MTV Video Music Awards, 60
Murphy, Eddie, 18–20, 38, 44, 56, 61

## N

National Association for the Advancement of Colored People (NAACP), 65
new material, 54
New York City, 31, 32, 34, 37, 40, 54, 61, 77
*Night School*, 81–82, 85

Nokia Theater, 57
*North Hollywood*, 40

## O

observational comedy, 28
on the road, 43
opening up onstage, 54–56

## P

*Paper Soldiers*, 39
Parrish, Eniko (wife), 6, 73, 74–76
Philadelphia, Pennsylvania, 6, 9, 10, 11, 21, 26, 29, 33, 41, 49, 79, 83, 87
pitching products, 86
Plastic Cup Boyz, 57
political issues, 79–80
producer, 87
Pryor, Richard, 31, 56, 73

## R

*Real Husbands of Hollywood*, 63–65
*Ride Along*, 6, 67
*Ride Along 2*, 68, 80
Robinson, Keith, 29–33, 34, 35
Roc-A-Fella Records, 38
Rock, Chris, 27, 38, 51, 61, 69, 73

# Index

## S
*Saturday Night Live*, 20, 38, 69–70
*Scary Movie 3*, 41
second-highest-paid comedian, 82
*Secret Life of Pets, The*, 82
*Secret Life of Pets 2, The*, 82
Seinfeld, Jerry, 28, 73, 83
*Seriously Funny*, 50–52
shoe salesman, 6, 21, 22
significant loss, 49–50
social media, 48–49, 52
*Soul Plane*, 42
stand-up comedy, 20, 23, 25, 26, 36, 47, 52, 61, 63, 77, 79
Stand Up NY, 34
stand-up tour, 44

## T
taking a chance, 26–27
taking a risk, 56–59
*Think Like a Man*, 59–60
*Think Like a Man Too*, 69
*TIME* magazine, 71, 73
*Top Five*, 69
troubled father, 12–14

## U
*Undeclared*, 40
unhappy marriage, 46–47
United Negro College Fund (UNCF), 72
universal appeal, 79, 85
Universal Studios, 85
urban comedian, 66

## W
What Now? tour, 77–79, 83
Witherspoon, Henry (father), 10, 13, 53, 54
  addiction, 12
  new relationship with, 14–15
  working on his act, 32–33
worth, 82–83
writing own material, 41–42

## About the Author

Carla Mooney is a graduate of the University of Pennsylvania. Today, she writes for young people and is the author of many books for young adults and children. Mooney is a fan of pop culture and comedy and enjoys learning the story behind today's hottest entertainment stars.

## Photo Credits

Cover, p. 3 lev radin/Shutterstock.com; cover background, interior pages (curtain) Kostsov/Shutterstock.com; p. 7 Matt Winkelmeyer/Getty Images; p. 11 f11 photo/Shutterstock.com; p. 15 Danny Moloshok/REUTERS/Newscom; p. 17 Michael Kovac/WireImage/Getty Images; p. 19 Ron Galella/Getty Images; p. 24 The Washington Post/Getty Images; p. 28 Cindy Ord/Getty Images; p. 30 Bobby Bank/WireImage/Getty Images; p. 32 Oliver Morris/Hulton Archive/Getty Images; p. 36 Michael Boardman/WireImage/Getty Images; p. 37 George Pimentel/WireImage/Getty Images; p. 39 Ray Tamarra/Getty Images; p. 42 Entertainment Pictures/Alamy Stock Photo; p. 45 Maury Phillips/WireImage/Getty Images; p. 46 Gabriel Olsen/Getty Images; p. 51 Phil Bray/© Screen Gems/courtesy Everett Collection; p. 60 Kevin Mazur/WireImage/Getty Images; p. 62 Ethan Miller/Getty Images; p. 64 Kevin Winter/Getty Images; p. 68 Moviestore collection Ltd/Alamy Stock Photo; pp. 70, 72 © AP Photo; p. 75 Tinseltown/Shutterstock.com; pp. 78, 84 Gilbert Carrasquillo/Getty Images; p. 81 Lifestyle pictures/Alamy Stock Photo.

Design and Layout: Nicole Russo-Duca; Editor: Siyavush Saidian; Photo Researcher: Sherri Jackson